The Armies of 1 Schleswig-Holstein war 1848-51

by
Ralph Weaver

With illustrations by Ralph Weaver

tional Illustrations taken from *Soldaterliv* by JHelms (published 1883), *Felttogene* by F Holst & A Larson (published 1888), *Das Ehrenkleid des Soldaten* by M Lezius (published 1936) and *Uniformenkunde* by R Knötel (published 1890-1921)

PARTIZAN PRESS

Published by Partizan Press 2007
816 - 818 London Road, Leigh-on-sea,
Essex, SS9 3NH
Ph/Fx: +44 (0) 1702 473986
Email: ask@caliverbooks.com
www.caliverbooks.com

First published in Great Britain in 2007 by
Partizan Press

Design & Production by Jay Forster
(www.generate.me.uk)

ISBN: 978-1-85818-499-9

Printed in the UK by Haynes Publishing

Front Page:
Schleswig-Holstein, Jaeger in full and field dress
© *Ralph Weaver*

Previous Page:
Danish Hussar on Outpost Duty
© *Ralph Weaver*

Back Page:
See pages 49-56 for descriptions.
All © Ralph Weaver

PARTIZAN HISTORICAL TITLES:

PARTIZAN SPECIAL EDITION SERIES:

PARTIZAN ARMY GUIDES SERIES:

PARTIZAN BATTLEDRESS SERIES:

PARTIZAN PRESTIGE FORMAT (hardback):

PARTIZAN CLASSICS SERIES:

PARTIZAN PRESS WARGAME RULES:

CONTENTS

Forward

This book grew from a casual conversation with Dave Ryan of Caliver Books who said to me, choose your own subject! What a gift! I have been involved with the history of the wars of continental Europe for many years, firstly as part of a study group within the Victorian Military Society and latterly as a member of the Continental Wars Society.

The subject for this book sprang from a long, and continuing, correspondence with Stuart Penhall a military history enthusiast and wargamer who lives on the outskirts of Sydney. He has been researching the Danish-German wars for some time and has built up a number of contacts both by letter and by the wonders of the internet in Denmark and Germany. I owe him a debt of thanks for supplying me with much difficult to find information which he has freely shared. My thanks also to John Pocock for reading the text and suggesting amendments for the sake of clarity. However, the end result is my responsibility and I take full blame for any errors.

I must say now that much of the history of the war is unrecorded or lies in some vault in obscure Danish or German libraries. What is gathered here is, I hope, sufficient to provide a basic knowledge of the armies involved in the war. As in many conflicts, especially in the nineteenth century, armies were changing the style of their uniforms and 1848 was no exception. Hence some of the comments on a particular state's uniform appear to be less than definite. Official regulations are one thing, without written or pictorial evidence it is not possible to be sure and sometimes, even where evidence does exist it is contradictory.

This book is not about the war itself so I have deliberately restricted the story of the campaign of each year to a single page otherwise this book would double in size.

Ralph Weaver
2006

Notes on names.

The duchy of Schleswig had a mixed population and as a result many places and natural features had both Danish and German versions of their name (Dybbøl and Düppel). Both languages also have letters and accents unknown in English which alter the sound of the letters. I have tried to use the common form of a name, which because the duchy was under German sovereignty for most of the time, tends to be the German name. This is not intended to be derogatory to Danish speakers, but to make it easier to understand for English readers.

With Holstein we are on firmer ground as German names are almost universal.

When we get into Jutland the names will be purely Danish. However I have used the English name where it is better known, for example Copenhagen for Kjøbenhavn and Jutland for Jydland.

Where possible I have avoided the German umlaut (double dots above a vowel) and used the now more accepted German usage of adding an 'e' to the word, jaeger for jäger.

Chapter 1
An accident waiting to happen

In many parts of Europe in the nineteenth century, as now, national boundaries did not always follow ethnic lines. There were German speakers in France; Italians in Austria; and Poles in Russia, Austria and Prussia! In the southern lands of the Danish kingdom there existed the three duchies of Holstein, Lauenburg and Schleswig. These had a large German speaking population, but with a mixture of people who considered themselves Danes, especially in the northern parts of Schleswig. Apart from Lauenburg, which had come to Denmark after the Treaty of Vienna in 1815, this situation had existed since the Middle Ages and the only bone of contention was who would rule the duchies, the Danish monarchy or local German princes, which had long been settled on the reigning king of Denmark. The two duchies of Schleswig and Holstein had their own parliaments (termed Estates, in effect a council of nobles) to run internal affairs under the overall authority of the Danish government sitting in Copenhagen.

The French revolution and the Napoleonic wars changed the European political and social climate utterly. Many of the old monarchies were swept away and those which remained had to modify the way they treated their subjects, agreeing to more political rights and freedoms. After 1815 nationalism became an important political factor in Europe and in the duchies this was seen as not just the limited interest of being a Holsteiner or Schleswiger, but the greater idea of being 'German'. They began to consider themselves as Germans living under a foreign sovereign. By the 1830's national and linguistic arguments brought the situation to the fore, also affecting the government in Copenhagen. Here two schools of thought were in conflict, the 'National Liberals' who wanted to incorporate Schleswig into the Danish monarchy proper and give Holstein some form of autonomy or federal status and the conservatives who wished to maintain the existing situation.

To complicate matters even further, Holstein was a member of the Germanic Confederation (an organisation set up after 1815 to look after the interests of all the German states and dominated by Austria) while Schleswig was not. Many leading German inhabitants of the duchies came to see the answer to their problems as the amalgamation of the duchies under their own ruler and for the new state to become a member of the Confederation.

The year 1848 was a dramatic one for Europe with the revolution in Paris followed by similar uprisings by the populace in Berlin and Vienna, a revolt in Hungary against the rule of the Austrian Hapsburgs, war in Italy and revolutions in Baden and Saxony. In mid March a meeting was convened in Rendsburg by the Schleswig and Holstein members of their parliaments which resulted in decision to send a deputation to the king to press their claims.

This brought about a revolution in Copenhagen with the 'National Liberals' forcing the king to dismiss the government and appoint their own supporters in their place. The National Liberal's policy was not to give in to the Schleswig-Holsteiners and to use force if necessary to restore Danish authority in the duchies. The immediate reaction was the proclamation of a Provisional government in the duchies under the leadership of Prince Frederick of Schleswig-Holstein-Sonderborg-Augustenburg-Noer, (referred to hereafter as the prince of Noer) who had some claim to the throne of the duchies.

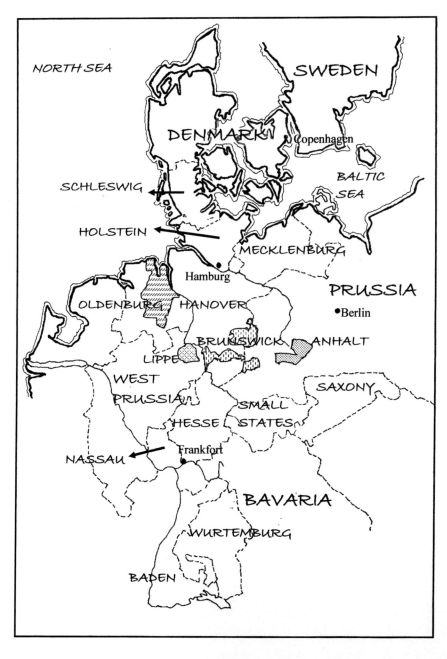

Chapter 2
Opening moves

The new Provisional government of Schleswig-Holstein realised that on its own it could not hope to maintain its integrity against the much larger Danish state and army. It needed allies. The first task of the Prince of Noer was to get help, so he visited Berlin to enlist Prussian aid. At that time Berlin was convulsed by a revolution of its own, but the Prussian king, Frederick William IV, saw an opportunity of placating his own radicals by offering to support the Schleswig-Holsteiners in their fight for national recognition. It was agreed that a Prussian division of 12,000 men under General Wrangel would enter the duchies, to support the uprising and possibly take the fight beyond the borders and invade the Jutland peninsula itself. At the same time an appeal to the German Federal Parliament sitting in Frankfort, brought the promise of a Federal division of 10,000 men made up of contingents from Hanover, Mecklenburg, and Brunswick. More immediately the arrival of 50 officers from Prussia helped relieve the shortage in the Schleswig-Holstein battalions.

On the very day (March 24th) that the proclamation of independence was read out from the town hall in Kiel, a special train containing the garrison of Kiel (250 men of the 5th Jaegers on the Danish establishment, later renumbered 2nd Jaegers in the Schleswig-Holstein army) together with 50 men of the Civic Guard, set out for Rendsburg. The Prince of Noer led this little army and its intention was to take over the arsenal with its military stores. The plan was have the garrison to parade without arms so sympathizers in Rendsburg arranged for a fire drill to take place, all the troops falling in on the parade ground (which still exists). At that time the railway ran through the town to a station within the fortress; with the troops waiting on parade the Prince of Noer arrived with his armed escort and had the Proclamation read out, exhorting the garrison to join him. To a man they did, the officers however declined and were given safe conduct out of the city. The stores found within the arsenal did not quite come up to expectations, most of the weapons were old, but there was plenty of artillery and enough money was found in the 'war-chest' to pay for the new army's weapons, uniforms and equipment.

While this was taking place, a new government had been formed in Copenhagen, controlled by the 'National Liberals'. The new War Minister, Anthon Tscherning, a former captain of artillery, quickly reorganised the Danish army. He now became the actual commander of the army instead of the king. Tscherning made two crucial appointments, Colonel Christoph Hedemann was promoted to Major-General and commander in chief with Captain Verner Læssøe as chief of staff. The 36 year old captain was a supporter of the National Liberals and just happened to be one of the most competent officers in the army.

The new Danish high command quickly formulated a plan to disperse the Schleswig-Holstein forces and take back control of the duchies. Hedemann with the 7,000 men of the 'North Jutland Corps', was to march south from Kolding while a second formation, the 'Flank Corps', 3,800 men under Colonel Schleppegrell was to cross to the mainland from the island of Alsen. They should be strong enough to defeat the much smaller and still disorganised forces of the duchies.

But before the Danish plan could be put into action the Provisional Government decided that they must, for political reasons, take the initiative.

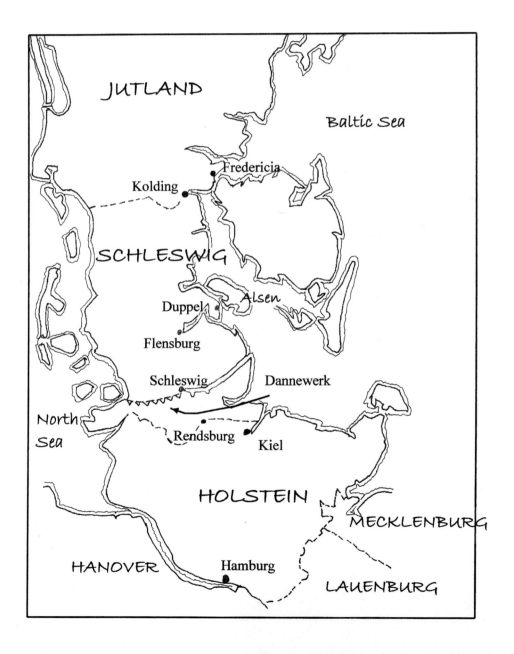

Chapter 3
The Danish Army

The Danish army in 1848 was based on the Army Act of 1842, which reorganised the existing forces. The rank and file were conscripted from among the peasants with the officers drawn from the educated gentry. Soldiers served for four years in the 'standing army' with a further four years in the war reserve. All soldiers remained liable for duty in the 'reinforcements' up to the age of 45. These latter troops initially existed on paper only and it was not till later in the war that 'reinforcement' battalions were activated. At the outbreak of hostilities most Danish units were considerably under strength.

The infantry were organised into battalions, one of The Royal Foot Guard, 17 of infantry and five of light infantry (jaegers). The cavalry was made up of one squadron of Horse Guards, two of Guard Hussars and six dragoon regiments each of four squadrons. The artillery had two regiments each of six batteries.

Much equipment was held in the arsenals in Holstein, which was intended to equip the Holstein contingent to the Germanic Confederation. As this fell into the hands of the Schleswig-Holsteiners at the beginning of the war, the Danish army had to fall back on the weapons held in the Royal Arsenal in Copenhagen. The result was that the most common weapons were the smooth bore muzzle loading muskets M.1822 and M.1828. Both were converted from flint to percussion lock. The jaegers were issued with a percussion rifle, the model M.1831. This was constructed on the 'pillar breech' principle where the conical bullet when rammed hard sat on a pillar protruding from the base of the barrel which forced the bullet to fit tightly into the bore. These weapons were used to replace the earlier muskets during the course of the war, supplemented with muskets purchased from France.

The cavalry were poorly armed; besides sabres they had flintlock carbines and pistols. In 1849 large numbers of percussion carbines and pistols were bought from Belgium.

The artillery of the Danish army was based on the 'System 1834'. This standardised the carriages and limbers for ease of production and maintenance. A light field battery had eight guns, six six-pounder guns and two 12 pounder howitzers; heavy batteries had 12 pounder guns and 24 pounder howitzers. The system also included an 84 pounder howitzer which was used as a siege gun and as fortress artillery.

At the beginning of hostilities the Danes could field about 12,000 men.

The order of battle during the early part of April 1848 was as follows:

Commander Major   General von Hedemann
Chief of staff   Captain Læssøe

Advance Guard   Lt-Colonel von Magius
    12th Line Battalion
    3rd Jaegers
    Hussars, two squadrons
    Artillery, four 6 pounders

1st Infantry Brigade   Colonel von Bülow
    1st Line Battalion
    2nd Line Battalion
    11th Line Battalion
    3rd Dragoons, one squadron
    Artillery detachment two guns

2nd Infantry Brigade   Colonel von Meyer
    4th Line Battalion
    7th Line Battalion
    5th Dragoons, one squadron
    Artillery detachment, four 6 pounder guns

Flank Corps   Colonel von Schleppegrell
    5th Line Battalion
    9th Line Battalion
    10th Line Battalion
    1st Jaegers
    2nd Jaegers
    4th Dragoons, one and a half squadrons
    Artillery detachment, six 6 pounder guns

Cavalry Brigade   Major General von Wedel-Wedelsborg
    3rd Dragoons three squadrons
    6th Dragoons, four squadrons
    Artillery detachment, four six pounders

Reserve   Colonel von Juel
    Battalion Foot Guards
    13th Line Battalion (under strength as recruited in Schleswig)
    5th Dragoons, three squadrons
    14 guns (mixed 6 and 12 pounders)

Uniforms 1848

Line battalions

The Army Act of 1842 also brought standardisation to the army. Up till then the regiments had red coatees with various coloured facings. From 1842 all battalions wore light blue facings. However in 1848 the Danish army was planning to modernise and make further major changes to its uniforms. The 1848 designs had been approved and officers had begun to appear in front of their companies in the new style with privately made uniforms. The infantry battalions did not look very different from their Napoleonic forebears, in black shakos and red tail coats.

The official uniform consisted of a black felt shako, with leather top and peak and decorated with two metal strips which held the Danish national cockade of a red disk within a white circle. A small white plume was worn above the cockade. Below the cockade, a white metal disc bearing the battalion number. At the back of the shako a small leather neck cloth held in place by two small buttons.

The red double breasted coatee introduced in 1842 had two rows of eight white metal buttons, the tails having white turnbacks. The front of the coatee was piped white and the collar, cuffs and shoulder straps were light blue piped white, with the battalion number in white on the shoulder straps. The cuffs were closed by two smaller white metal buttons.

The trousers were light blue and worn loose over the shoes and gaiters. In bad weather the trousers could be rolled up into large cuffs.

White crossbelts supported a black leather ammunition pouch and a short, slightly curved sword and bayonet. Attached to the ammunition pouch crossbelt was a small natural leather pouch holding the percussion caps. A second smaller ammunition pouch was sometimes worn on the front of the black waistbelt. A bread bag and tin waterbottle were also included in the soldier's equipment. Spare clothing and shoes were carried in a brown hide backpack supported on red straps. A grey blanket roll/greatcoat was attached to the top of the pack. The greatcoat had red collar patches.

The shako was a cumbersome article and many soldiers wore the model 1842 field cap, similar to the Prussian round cap but with a small leather peak. The cap was light blue piped red with the Danish cockade on the head band. As part of the new uniform a kepi was introduced, called the Hungarian cap, and some individuals managed to get hold of them. It was light blue with a leather peak and chin strap, with a cockade and loop of cord in the national colours (red and white) held in place by a white metal button. The cords round the cap were white with red stripes. Officer's cords were silver with red stripes. Paintings show shakos, caps and kepis being worn in a single battalion.

Rank was denoted by a single inverted white lace chevron for lance corporal, two for a corporal, three for a sergeant and three with a white metal button for a sergeant major. Officers were distinguished by epaulettes and carried a sabre in a steel scabbard.

Many of the soldiers appeared clean shaven, but full beards were quite common among solders and officers.

Jaeger
The jaeger battalions had received their new uniforms in 1842. It was a double breasted dark green frock coat with red collar patches and piping down the front and round the pointed cuffs. White metal buttons. The collar patches were decorated with two white metal buttons with sewn button holes. Trousers were also dark green. The 1842 field cap was dark green with red piping and a Danish cockade on the front. All belts and pouches were black leather, apart from the pack straps which were red as in the line battalions. Side arms consisted of a short 'Roman' style sword and a bayonet.

Artillery
The artillery uniform was the same as the line infantry but with dark blue facings and yellow metal buttons. Yellow metal fittings to the shako. Sidearm was a short sabre in a black leather scabbard with yellow metal fittings.

Foot Guard battalion
The Guard battalion followed the dress of the line battalions, but the headgear was a black bearskin with a small peak and a large white metal 'sun ray' plate. Trousers were light blue with a white stripe. The red coatee had a single bar of white lace on the collar and cuffs and the sovereign's monogram in white on the shoulder straps. Contemporary pictures however, show the Foot Guard in the new dark blue tunic right from the start of the war. The Napoleonic period cartridge pouch was retained, black leather with the sovereign's coat of arms in the centre of the flap and a flaming grenade in each corner all in white metal. White cross belts held together with an oval white metal plate.

Dragoons
The distinctive dragoon headdress was a black leather helmet, not unlike a 'pickelhaube' shape, but with a high brass classical style comb. It was reinforced with two brass strips either side of the chinscale bosses and had a large brass plate on the front with a raised sunburst badge. Brass edging to the front and back peaks and brass chinscales. On the left side of the helmet, above the chinscale boss, a red, edged white, cockade. The red double breasted coatee had a light blue collar, pointed cuffs and shoulder straps bearing the regimental number in white. White waistbelt supporting a heavy

Denmark, Officers of Engineers 1848 (dark blue uniform, black facings and red piping)

Denmark, Artilleryman 1848

sabre with a brass hilt carried in a steel scabbard. White shoulder belts with cartridge pouch and carbine. Some pictures show plain light blue trousers, others light blue booted overalls, with black leather reinforced inside legs and false boots. The saddle cloth was light blue edged with two red strips. The dragoons were also supplied with a long red riding coat for winter wear.

Hussars

The two hussar squadrons were dressed in light blue dolman and trousers with white lace and piping. The pelisse was red with white lace and black fur lining. Shoulder belts white. The headwear was a black leather shako, tapering towards the top. White lace, cords and pompon. White metal shako plate. The sabratache was light blue edged with red in a 'vandyke' pattern, white piping and white crowned sovereign's initial *FR*. Red shabraque with pointed corners with blue 'vandyke' edging. The leather harness had a 'shell' decoration.

Lancers

Although the lancer squadrons had been disbanded in 1842, a troop was raised as orderlies. They wore the dragoon uniform, but retained the lancer chapka. This cap was also worn by a volunteer unit of hussars. The body of the cap was black leather with a red cloth covered top. The peak, chinscales and cap plate were brass, the pompon white and the cords and flounders white with crimson stripes. This unit wore black leather sabretaches.

Horse Guards

Unlike the dragoons and hussars the Horse Guards took no part in the fighting. They were still dressed in the old cuirassier style with yellow coatees with red collar with two white lace bars and brass breast and back plates. Black pouch belt and waist belt carrying a long straight sword and black leather sabretache. White breaches and knee length riding boots. Red shabraque edged with two white stripes. The black leather helmet had a brass comb with black fur crest and brass plate and chinscales.

Volunteers

Most Danes joined the regular or reinforcement battalions, but a few men formed volunteer units at the outbreak of hostilities. They were generally of company strength, on average about 150 men. They were raised by local communities as a home guard to protect themselves against what they thought would be an invasion of German 'bandits and criminals'. The companies were generally attached to regular battalions.

By the end of June 1848 most units were amalgamated into the 1st Battalion of Danish Volunteers. In August the battalion was disbanded and the troops distributed as additional companies to the regular battalions.

There were several units of militia in the larger towns, the Copenhagen militia served as part of the capital's garrison and the Kolding militia guarded German prisoners in the town jail.

Uniforms 1849

Line battalions
The new uniform to be introduced in 1848/9 was a dark blue, full skirted double breasted tunic with self coloured collar and cuffs. The front of the coat, rear skirts and false pocket flaps, cuffs and shoulder straps were decorated with red piping. The collar had a red patch on each side with two buttons with decorated button holes. The battalion number was shown in red on the shoulder straps. The straps and equipment were intended to be black leather, but as it took some time to re-equip the battalions, the old white cross belts and red pack straps continued to be worn for some time. The light blue trousers were retained in the new uniform. The old, heavy shako was replaced by the 'Hungarian' kepi mentioned above. Officers carried a sabre in a steel scabbard with a gold sword knot with red strips. Silver shoulder cords

Jaegers
See above, the jaegers already wore the new style uniform when hostilities broke out.

Artillery
The style for the artillery was the same as the line battalions, dark blue tunic with red piping on the coat front and cuffs. The collar patches were crimson and the buttons yellow metal. Trousers were also dark blue as was the kepi. The kepi cords were yellow with red stripes, officers gold cords on kepi and shoulders. The equipment was intended to be black leather, but as in the line battalions, it took some time to for supplies to come through. In the interim the former white belts were retained. A brass hilted short sword was carried in a black leather scabbard.

Foot Guard battalion
The new tunic had two silver lace bars on each collar patch and one on each cuff. The bearskin was retained as before. The light blue trousers had wide white stripes. The position with equipment was the same for the line, so the old white cross belts were worn until the new black belts could be issued.

Dragoons
The only change was the introduction of the dark blue infantry tunic, but with crimson collar patches. Officers had double crimson stripes on the trousers.

Danish drill sergeant.

Danish hussars on patrol

Hussars

The hussars retained their former uniform.

Musicians

Drummers and buglers in the infantry were distinguished by 'swallow's nests in red with white zigzag lace. Jaegers wore similar and dragoons crimson with white lace. The drums were not as deep as the Napoleonic period, but deeper than those adopted by the Prussians at this time. The shells were brass and the wooden rims painted with red and white vandyking. The jaeger bugles were held on white/red/green cords.

Flags

The Danish regimental standards consisted of a red sheet with the white Danish cross in the centre, the arms of the cross widening until they reached the edges. In the top quarter, next to the pole, was placed the monogram of the monarch in whose reign the flag was presented, Christian VIII (CVIII) or Frederick VII (FVII) and in the lower quarter the regimental number also in Latin characters (the 9th Regiment had 'IX') all in gold. In the bottom fly quarter the letters KR for a reserve battalion and FB for a reinforcement battalion. All cords and tassels in yellow/gold. The Foot Guard battalion had a similar red and white cross, but with the sovereign's monogram (C VIII) and a crown in the centre of the arms of the cross.

Chapter 4
The Schleswig-Holstein army

The Army in 1848

In March 1848 the Provisional Government of the duchies had no troops to call upon to support the revolt against the army mustering in Copenhagen. However Schleswig-Holsteiners formed a large part of the battalions stationed in the duchies and almost all the rank and file supported the new government, while the officers were split, most adhering to their oath of loyalty the Danish king. As a result the new units formed in Schleswig-Holstein were chronically short of suitable officer material. About a quarter of the regular Danish army sided with the Provisional government. These formed the basis of the forces of the duchies who struggled against the Danish army for three years. New units were formed who were incorporated into the Schleswig-Holstein army and support came from all over Germany as volunteers rushed to help their fellow countrymen against the Danes.

At first the Schleswig-Holstein battalions were just the renumbered Danish battalions, the Danish 14th battalion became the 1st Schleswig-Holstein battalion; the 15th, the 2nd; the 16th the 3rd and the 17th the 4th battalion. The 5th and 6th Battalions were newly raised units and did not have old Danish battalion numbers. The Danish 4th and 5th jaegers became the 1st and 2nd Schleswig-Holstein jaegers. The volunteers formed 'Freikorps' companies, such as the Students and Gymnast's Club company, who were young men from political clubs with strong revolutionary ideals. In just a few days four units numbering 1,000 men were organised.

The 1st and 2nd Danish dragoon regiments became the 1st and 2nd Schleswig-Holstein dragoon regiments. The Danish 2nd Artillery regiment became in effect the Schleswig-Holstein artillery.

As most of the troops came from the Danish regular forces, arms and equipment started out similar. Enough artillery was captured from the arsenal at Rendsburg to equip the Schleswig-Holstein army for the whole of the war, although draught horses were a problem. As the army was rapidly expanded the cash from the arsenal was used by agents for the Schleswig-Holstein government to buy arms from neighbouring countries. 6,000 muskets came from depots in Berlin and Magdeburg (Prussian percussion model 1839, converted from 1809 flintlocks). Orders were placed in Solingen (a steel making town, the German equivalent of Sheffield) for 800 cavalry sabres, 1,200 artillery side arms and 1,600 infantry short swords.

In 1849 further orders were given to factories in Liege, Solingen and Suhl (a town in Prussia noted in medieval times for the manufacture of weapons and armour and in the nineteenth century for high quality firearms) for cavalry, artillery and infantry officer's swords, 13,500 infantry short swords and bayonets and 17,000 muskets. Many of these newly made weapons were of such good standard that they were taken over by the Danish army in 1851 and were used against the Austrians and Prussians during the Second Schleswig War in 1864!

The order of battle on 3rd April 1848 was:

1st Brigade,   Major General von Krohn

1st Battalion	510 men
3rd Battalion	673 men
5th Jaegerkorps	473 men (note, still retaining the Danish numbering)
Volunteers	225 men

2nd Brigade,   Major General Duke Charles of Schleswig-Holstein-Sonderburg-Gluecksburg

2nd Battalion	577 men
4th Battalion	816 men
Unassigned	200 men
4th Jaegerkorps	749 men (note, still retaining the Danish numbering)
Volunteers	280 men
1st Dragoons	220 men
2nd Dragoons	334 men
Artillery	2 batteries 16 guns and 180 men

Forming:

5th Battalion	900 men
6th Battalion	500 men
Mounted volunteers	100 men
Dismounted dragoons	400 men

Total strength: 6,957 men

The volunteer force was looked upon very seriously and within days of the forming of the Provisional Government a 'Freikorps' command was set up under Lieutenant Colonel Koch. As Prussian officers arrived in Schleswig-Holstein to make up the deficiency, the leadership of the volunteers was taken over by Captain von Gersdorff of the Garde Schuetzen Battalion from Berlin.

By 10th April the volunteers had been organised into the 1st, 2nd and 3rd Freikorps. The 1st under von Krogh had five companies, the 2nd commanded by Count von Rantzau, six companies and the 3rd under

Captain von Wasmer, four companies. A 4th Freikorps was added to the list under the Bavarian Major von der Tann (later general in 1866 and 1870). This was to become the focus for volunteers from all over Germany. By May it consisted of six companies and in July it was reorganised into two battalions each of four companies, an artillery detachment of two 6 pounder guns and two howitzers, a mounted troop of 32 men and an engineer detachment. Many former soldiers fought within its ranks.

Two volunteer units achieved special status, Bracklow's Volunteer Sharpshooters became an independent unit and from May was considered to be part of the regular Schleswig-Holstein army. The men all came from the best families in the duchies and brought their own uniforms and rifles. The only mounted unit, the Eiderstedt Mounted Guard, a group of peasant volunteers, was chosen by the Prince of Noer as his body guard and were later used as messengers.

Uniforms

The ex-members of the royal Danish army brought their existing uniforms with them, but they could not appear in the field looking the same as their enemies. The easiest way to differentiate the Schleswig-Holsteiners from the Danes was to adopt the undress or working uniform, this was a short, light blue, single breasted jacket, without tails, with a red collar. Light blue trousers and black shoes. Standard Danish equipment included the pack with red straps. The light blue peaked field cap had red piping round the band and peak. A similar working jacket, a double breasted grey garment with white metal buttons was also worn. The jaeger units already had the new Danish uniforms, so a white band was added to the upper left arm.

Some units were clothed in Prussian uniforms, dark blue tunic piped red. Red patches on the blue collar. Grey trousers piped red. The Prussian pack and equipment was used including the greatcoat worn in a roll over the left shoulder. White arm bands were worn by many units for identification.

The volunteers had no uniforms at first, and many units disappeared before any could be organised. Some, such as the Kiel Student's and Gymnasts Corps adopted an off-white worker's type blouse with either open neck showing shirt collar and tie, or buttoned up with a turned down collar. Light grey trousers. The one thing they shared was a high crowned soft hat with a wide brim turned up on either side. Moustaches and beards were common. Arms and equipment varied from man to man, anything from flintlocks to shotguns to pistols. Bracklow's Sharpshooters wore a grey tunic with green collar and piping and grey trousers. Dark green slouch hat with a black feather. All straps and belts were black leather. Most volunteers adopted a cockade in the 'German' revolutionary colours of red, black and gold, but Bracklow's men, favouring a royal form of government, used the Schleswig-Holstein colours of red, white and blue. Volunteer officers and standard bearers (where they had them) wore a black/red/yellow sash, apart from the 6th company of the 4th Freikorps, who, to show their political sympathies, wore red! Von der Tann himself seems to have retained his Bavarian uniform and the commander of the Eiderstedt Mounted Guard wore the uniform of his regiment of Prussian hussars

One of the company's in von der Tann's Freikorps, made up of volunteers from Prussia, came dressed in green blouses and tall kepis, similar to the ones worn by the French chasseurs. A group from Reuss, one of the smallest German states, wore white linen uniforms with leather helmets (probably pickelhaube as the Reuss regulars had already adopted such a helmet). The 30 men from Brunswick arrived ready uniformed in dark blue coats and trousers, with a cap covered in black bearing a silver skull and the motto 'Für Deutschland' (For Germany). The duke of Schwarzburg-Rudolstadt provided his contingent with green coats and black pickelhaube helmets.

The volunteers as a whole chose whatever military style they considered suitable, including large hats, high leather boots, waist sashes, etc. Many individuals adopted the black/red/gold cockade on their headgear and some sported a skull and crossbones.

Feverish activity on behalf of the Provincial Government produced designs of a new 'German' style uniform, strongly based on the Prussian model. For the line battalions this was a dark blue single breasted tunic with red collar, red piping and pointed red cuffs. The white shoulder straps had the battalion number in red. White metal buttons. Light blue trousers with red piping. The headwear was a black leather pickelhaube with squared front peak. The spike and metal fittings were all yellow metal, including a double headed eagle front plate with the arms of Schleswig-Holstein. A Schleswig-Holstein cockade was worn under the chinscale boss on the right side (blue/white/red) and a 'German' cockade on the left (black/red/gold). For undress a round field cap with a blue top, piped red and a red band.

A white waist belt carried a black cartridge pouch at the front and a short brass hilted 'roman' style sword on the left side. The brown pack was supported on white straps. A white bread bag and small waterbottle completed the equipment. Grey Prussian style greatcoats were worn.

Drummers and buglers had red swallow's nests in the Prussian fashion.

The jaeger battalions were ordered to wear the same style of uniform, but in green with red facings and piping and dark grey trousers with red piping. Instead of the helmet a tall black shako with leather front and back peaks and a yellow metal double headed eagle plate and a long drooping black horsehair plume. Cockades as for the infantry helmet. The plume was not just for parade but was worn in the field as well. A green field cap with red band and piping was worn in undress. Black leather equipment.

Schleswig-Holstein artillery

Artillery

The artillery adopted the same style of uniform as the infantry, a dark blue tunic with crimson collar, shoulder straps and pointed cuffs and piping and yellow metal buttons. The trousers were light blue with red piping. The helmet was topped with a ball instead of the infantry spike. All straps were white leather. The side arm was a short, slightly curved sabre with brass fittings carried in a black leather scabbard from the waistbelt. Brown cowhide pack with steel mess tin.

Pioneers

They wore the artillery uniform, however the collar and cuffs were black piped in red, the shoulder straps dark blue piped white. Black leather belts and straps, side arm a special pioneer sword.

Train

The Train were responsible for ammunition supply to the artillery and infantry and wore the infantry tunic in dark blue with light blue collar, cuffs and piping. Light blue riding trousers piped red and with the inside re-enforced with black leather. Steel spurs. They only wore the round field cap in dark blue with a light blue band and piping. Arms were a dragoon sabre.

Dragoons

Cornflower blue tunic and riding trousers, carmine collar, cuffs and piping. White shoulder straps with regiment number in red. White metal buttons. The helmet was steel with brass fittings. White belts. Arms were a sabre with a steel hilt and scabbard, a carbine and pistols. The saddle cloth was cornflower blue with carmine lace and piping.

Army in 1849

Reformed and re-organised the Schleswig-Holstein army on 1st January 1849 consisted of:

War Office
Army General Staff

Commander in chief: Lt General von Bonin (from Prussia)

1st Infantry Brigade: Colonel Count von Baudissin
  1st, 2nd, 3rd, 4th and 9th Infantry Battalions

2nd Infantry Brigade: Lt-Colonel von Sachau
  5th, 6th, 7th, 8th and 10th Infantry Battalions

Jaeger inspection: Lt-Colonel von Zastrow
  1st, 2nd, 3rd and 4th Jaeger Corps

Cavalry Brigade: Lt-Colonel von Fuersen-Bachmann
  1st and 2nd Dragoon regiments

Artillery regiment: Colonel Richter
  I st Field Artillery section:
  1st, 2nd and 3rd six pounder batteries
  II nd Field Artillery section:
  1st and 2nd 12 pounder batteries
  1 Horse artillery battery (forming)

Fortress artillery section with five batteries Major Liebert

Engineers Lt-Colonel von Dau
  Pontoon company
  Pioneer company

Transport company First Lieutenant Roehrig

Each infantry battalion had a Lt-Colonel or Major as commander plus six other headquarters staff. The four companies that made up the battalion were each commanded by a Captain, with a First Lieutenant and three Second Lieutenants. The company was made up of a Sergeant-Major, an Ensign (here an officer cadet with rank of sergeant-major), 18 sergeants, five

l-r: Danish - Foot Guard, Infantryman, Jaeger, Artillery

l-r: Danish - Hussar, Dragoon & Lifeguard

Danish infantry filling their waterbottles

Danish infantry firing from cover

Schleswig-Holstein army

Schleswig-Holstein jeagers

Schleswig-Holstein train and stretcher bearers of the jaegers

Schleswig-Holstein dragoons

signallers (three drummers and two buglers), 12 corporals and 188 musketeers. On paper a battalion consisted of 22 officers, 80 NCOs, 21 signallers and 752 men. In addition there were also two surgeons.

A dragoon regiment was commanded by a Colonel or Lt-Colonel, with eight staff. The five squadrons were each commanded by a captain, with one First Lieutenant, and three Second Lieutenants. The squadron was made up of a Sergeant-Major, a Cornet, 13 sergeants, three trumpeters, 12 corporals and 120 dragoons. Attached to each squadron was an assistant surgeon, a veterinarian, a smith and a saddler. At full strength a dragoon regiment totalled 28 officers, 65 NCOs 16 trumpeters, 60 corporals and 610 men.

An artillery battery consisted of a captain with a headquarters staff of 10 NCOs and men. The first half battery was commanded by a first lieutenant, the second half battery by a second lieutenant. The total strength of a battery was four sergeants, 12 bombardiers (corporals), 86 gunners, 68 drivers, 28 train soldiers and three trumpeters. In material there were six 6 pounder guns, two 12 pounder howitzers, eight munitions wagons, one spare limber, two forage wagons, one tool wagon, one wagon carrying the battery's packs, one bread wagon, one smith's wagon, and one wagon for the saddler and harness maker. This required 45 riding horses and 146 draught horses.

The Army in 1850

One year later there had been some changes to the Schleswig-Holstein army, based on the need to raise more troops.

Under the control of the Army Department was:

Army Command and General Staff

1st Infantry Brigade: Major-General Count von Baudissin
    1st, 2nd, 3rd, 4th and 9th Infantry Battalions

2nd Infantry Brigade: Colonel von Abercron
    5th, 6th, 7th, 8th and 10th Infantry Battalions

3rd Infantry Brigade: Colonel Fabricius
    11th, 12th, 13th, 14th and 15th Infantry Battalions

Jaeger Inspection: Colonel von Zastrow
    1st, 2nd, 3rd, 4th and 5th Jaeger Corps

Reserve brigade with cadres for:
    16th, 17th, 18th, 19th, 20th, 21st, 22nd and 23rd Infantry Battalions
    and 6th and 7th Jaeger Corps.

Cavalry Brigade:
    1st and 2nd Dragoon regiments

Artillery Brigade:
    I st Field Artillery section
    1st, 2nd and 4th six pounder batteries
    II nd Field Artillery section
    1st, 2nd and 3rd twelve pounder batteries
    III rd Field Artillery section
    Mounted battery and three 6 pounder gun batteries
        and one 24 pounder howitzer battery

Fortress Artillery;
    Six Fortress batteries

    Two pioneer companies

    Transport company

In 1851 Schleswig-Holstein had to stand alone against the Danes and the army was increased further. Under the Army Command there existed:

1st Infantry Brigade
    1st, 2nd, 3rd and 12th Infantry Battalions, 5th Jaeger Corps

2nd Infantry Brigade
    5th, 6th, 7th and 13th Infantry Battalions, 3rd Jaeger Corps

3rd Infantry Brigade
    9th, 10th and 11th Infantry Battalions, 1st and 4th Jaeger Corps

4th Infantry Brigade
    4th, 8th, 14th and 15th Infantry Battalions, 2nd Jaeger Corps

5th (Replacement) Infantry Brigade
    1st, 2nd and 3rd Replacement battalions

Cavalry Brigade:
    1st and 2nd Dragoon regiments

Artillery Brigade:
    I st Field Artillery section
    1st, 2nd 3rd and 5th six pounder batteries
    II nd Field Artillery section
    1st, 2nd and 3rd twelve pounder batteries
    III rd Field Artillery section
    Mounted battery, 1st and 2nd 24 pounder howitzer batteries
        and 4th 6 pounder battery

Fortress Artillery:
    Six Fortress batteries

| Schleswig-Holstein shore battery |

Flags

The newly formed battalions did not have regimental standards as did the Danes, but illustrations from the period generally show the German tricolour being used. This consisted of equal bands of black, red and gold. The flag is usually depicted with the stripes horizontally, with black at the top then red with gold (or yellow) at the bottom; although it is sometimes shown with the bands placed vertically with black next to the staff. The Schleswig-Holstein colours of (horizontal bands) blue, white and red do not seem to have been used in the field.

Two volunteer company standards have survived, the Kiel Student Corps carried a 'German' tricolour, but black top, gold centre and red at the bottom with gold fringes around three sides. The Aldosser company had a more usual black/red/gold with the words 'Gott mit Uns' (God is with Us) in white wool in the central red band and a dedication in the corners.

In camp the Schleswig-Holstein battalions had company marker flags, small swallow tailed sheets, white for the first company, red for the second, yellow for the third and blue for the fourth. There is no evidence that they were carried in the field.

Chapter 5
The Prussian Army

In 1848 the Prussian army did not have anything like the fearsome reputation it had by 1871. True it had been a formidable force under Frederick the Great, but by the end of his reign it had lost much of its vitality. Napoleon trounced it at the double battles of Jena and Auerstadt in 1806. In the long years of French domination it had slowly been brought back to efficiency by reforming officers such as Gniesenau, so that by 1815 it was once more a force to be reckoned with.

Wellington's strategy at Waterloo was to 'wait for the Prussians'. Indeed the reason why the last assault of the French infantry against the Allied line was so weak was that all Napoleon's reserves were fighting the ever increasing Prussian threat to his right wing. And it was the Prussian cavalry which lead the allied pursuit right to the gates of Paris.

After Napoleon's exile and death the Prussian army began to slip back into its old ways. Most of the non-noble officers who had brought new life to the army, were got rid of or just left in their junior ranks while others with the aristocratic 'von' in their name advanced. Though still a 'Great Power' in Europe, Prussia had to give precedence to Austria, Russia, England and later France.

When the revolution broke out in Paris in February of 1848, Berlin quickly followed suit, with barricades blocking the main streets and with the weapons from the Arsenal in the hands of the citizens of all classes. The royal government was rocked by the left wing sentiments of many of its people and saw intervention in Schleswig-Holstein against the Danes as an outlet to this 'German' (rather than Prussian) fervour.

A force was quickly got together, under General Wrangel, to send to Denmark. A further force was organised for the campaign in 1849 which included a large number of landwehr battalions. However as the landwehr at this time included a large 'liberal' element it was probably a good idea to get it out of the country for a while! The Landwehr organisation was set in 1813 to provide a territorial army to support the regular troops. After conscription a soldier would serve his time in the regular army and then in the reserve. After that he would enter the Landwehr, trained soldiers, but not in the first flush of youth!

Like the Federal X Corps the Prussian division was nominally under the orders of the Germanic parliament in Frankfort.

The Prussian troops assembled on 23rd April 1848 for the attack on the town of Schleswig consisted of:

Divisional commander: Lieutenant General Prince Radziwill

Left wing Brigade   Major General von Bonin

Advance Guard
    I R No. 31 (1 battalion)
    I R No. 20 (Fusilier battalion)
    part of Foot Battery No. 11 (2 guns)

Main body
    I R No. 2 (1st and 2nd Battalions)
    I R No. 12 (1st battalion)
    I R No. 20 (1st and 2nd battalions)
    part of Foot Battery No. 11
    part of Horse Battery No. 7
    Cuirassier Regiment No. 2

Right wing Brigade   Major General von Moellendorff

    Emperor Alexander of Russia Guard Grenadier Regiment (3 battalions)
    Emperor Franz of Austria Guard Grenadier Regiment (3 Battalions)
    Guard Rifle Battalion
    3rd Hussars
    Part of Guard Foot Artillery battery No. 3
    Part of Horse Artillery battery No. 7

Uniforms
While the prestige of the Prussian army was not of the highest, the fashion it set in the design of uniforms was widely copied within northern Germany and as its military prowess increased so did the spread of the 'pickelhaube' and its derivatives.

In 1843 Prussia introduced the tunic with coloured patches on the collar, coloured cuffs and piping. At the same time the spiked helmet made its appearance. The colour of the metal fittings and style of eagle plate was different for each branch of service. Initially the cross belts and pack straps from the old uniform were retained, but in 1848 a system designed by an officer named Virschow was introduced. The pack straps were fixed to the top of the pack, ran under the shoulder straps and finished in a metal clip which hooked under the waistbelt. This took the weight off the chest and onto the waist. Two small leather straps were fitted underneath the main straps and were buckled to the bottom of the pack to stop it bouncing while marching. A single ammunition pouch (later two) was hung on the front of the waistbelt and a short sword worn on the left side.

All Prussian line infantry had the same uniform, distinguished by different colour shoulder straps bearing the regimental number and cuff flap piping. The tunic was dark blue with red patches on either side of the dark blue collar and red piping down the front and on the rear skirts. Red cuffs and cuff flaps. Yellow metal buttons. Grey trousers piped red in winter and plain white for summer. Black shoes. Black leather spiked helmet with yellow metal eagle plate, spike and fittings and chinscales. A Prussian cockade of black/white/black was worn under the right chinscale boss and a German rosette of black/red/yellow on the left. The German cockade was worn between March 1848 and March 1851 only.

Regiment number	Shoulder straps	Regimental number	Cuff flap piping
1, 3, 4, 5, and 33	white	red	white
2, 9, 14, 21 and 34	white	red	none
8, 12, 20, 24 and 35	red	yellow	white
26, 27, 31, 32 and 36	red	yellow	none
6, 7, 18, 19 and 37	yellow	red	white
10, 11, 22, 23 and 38	yellow	red	none
13, 15, 16, 17 and 39	light blue	red	white
25, 28, 29, 30 and 40	light blue	red	none

The two musketeer battalions in each regiment (the 1st and 2nd) had white straps and waistbelt, with the third battalion (entitled 'Fusilier') black.

The two Guard Grenadier regiments wore a similar uniform to the Line but with two white lace loops on each collar patch. The Alexander regiment with white shoulder straps and red letter 'A' under a Russian style crown. The Franz regiment with red shoulder straps and yellow letter 'F' under an Austrian style crown. The eagle plate on the helmet was of a different style to the Line with spread wings. The Guard Rifle Battalion had a green tunic with black collar patches and cuffs all with red piping. At this period they wore a spiked helmet similar to other Prussian units.

On campaign officers wore a small version of the pack and had metal epaulettes without fringes and a silver sash with black threads running through it.

The needle gun had started its career in the Prussian army with the model of 1841, but the troops sent to Denmark were still armed with the Model M39 percussion muzzle loader.

Hussars
In 1843 the hussars took to wearing a black felt winged cap, similar in style to those worn in Frederick the Great's time. The wing was lined with coloured cloth. White horsehair plume for parade wear. However the 3rd

Hussars (along with the guard regiment) readopted the fur cap, with a red bag. In 1844 the 10th also took to wearing a fur cap and in 1850 all regiments were given them. Each regiment wore a dolman and pelisse of the same colour, including the collar and cuffs. White pouch belts. Dark grey riding trousers.

Regiment	Basic colour	Lace/buttons
Life Guard	blue (red dolman)	yellow
1st Life Hussars	black	white
2nd Life Hussars	black	white
3rd	blue (red dolman)	white
4th	brown	yellow
5th	red	white
6th	green	yellow
7th	black	yellow
8th	blue	white
9th	cornflower blue	yellow
10th	green	yellow
11th	green	white
12th	cornflower blue	white

It is not clear if the Prussians brought their regimental standards to Schleswig-Holstein, however as representatives of the German Confederation they are depicted in contemporary illustrations carrying the 'German' black/red/gold banner.

The Prussian colours consisted of a white sheet with a black maltese cross, in the centre of which was placed an orange disk surrounded by oak leaves and with a crown above. In the centre of the disk a Prussian black eagle clutching a sword in its right claws and thunderbolts in its left. In each corner of the sheet the sovereign's initials in gold surrounded by oak leaves and topped by a crown. In the centre of each of the black arms of the cross a bursting grenade.

Cuirassiers

The Prussian cuirassiers wore a white tunic, called a 'koller' of white material, closed with 14 concealed hooks and eyes. Collar patches, cuffs and piping in regimental colours, all with white lace. This colour was carried on to the pistol covers and saddle cloth. Steel cuirass and helmet with yellow metal fittings. Dark grey riding trousers piped red. White pouch belt. Long straight sword carried in a steel scabbard.

Regiment	Facing colour
Gardes du Corps	red
Guard Cuirassiers	cornflower blue
1st	black
2nd	carmine red
3rd	light blue
4th	orange
5th	rose red
6th	Russian blue
7th	lemon yellow
8th	light green

1849

Prussian 3rd Division of the Combined German Army, Maj General von Hirschfeld

I R No. 12 (3 battalions)
I R No. 15 (3 battalions
13th Landwehr Regiment (3rd Battalion)*
16th Landwehr Regiment (1st Battalion)*
17th Landwehr Regiment (1st Battalion)*
18th Landwehr Regiment (1st Battalion)**
19th Landwehr Regiment (1st and 3rd Battalions)**
7th Jaeger Battalion (three companies)

8th Hussars (four squadrons)
11th Hussars (four squadrons)
Engineer section (two companies)

Foot 6 pounder battery No. 4 (8 guns)
Foot 12 pounder battery No. 11 (6 guns)
Horse artillery battery no. 21 (8 guns)
Half battery of rockets (from the Austrian army)

*together the 'Combined Posen Regiment of Landwehr
** together the ' Combined Westphalian Regiment of Landwehr

Uniform

The Landwehr received the tunic in 1842 and to distinguish it from the Line infantry it dispensed with the piping down the front edge. Red collar patches, cuffs and cuff flaps. Shoulder straps and cuff flap piping was the same as the regular numbered regiment, the 13th, 16th and 17th had light blue shoulder straps and white cuff flap piping and the 18th and 19th yellow shoulder straps and white cuff flap piping. The helmet was the same as the Line with the addition of a white metal landwehr cross on the breast of the eagle plate. The equipment was also similar save only that the Landwehr usually wore a single cartridge pouch on the waist belt at the back.

The artillery also wore the dark blue tunic, with black collar patches and cuffs (round cuffs for the Horse artillery) all piped in red. The helmet was as the infantry, but by 1849 the top of the spike was replaced by a ball. Red shoulder straps. All belts and straps were white leather. The Austrian Rocket troops wore the artillery uniform of brown tailed coatee with red collar, cuffs and turnbacks and yellow metal buttons. The trousers were light blue. White belts. Hat with brim turned up on the left, yellow and black cockade with black over yellow plume.

The Landwehr standard was as the Line, but colours reversed so that it appeared as a white cross on a black ground and without the bursting grenade emblems.

Prussia, Drummer, Emperor Franz of Austria Guard Grenadier Regiment

Chapter 6
The Federal German Army

The German parliament sitting in Frankfurt had no troops of its own and it responded to the call for help from Schleswig-Holstein by mobilising that part of the Germanic Federation forces nearest to the duchies, in this case the Federal X Corps provided by the kingdom of Hanover, Duchy of Brunswick, Duchy of Oldenburg and the Grand Duchy of Mecklenburg-Schwerin. The contingents were not the whole armies of the various states, but the number to be contributed in relation to their populations.

Hanover had to contribute up to 13,000 men and 26 guns and formed the 1st Division.

Mecklenburg-Schwerin contributed 2,000 men, infantry, cavalry and artillery which were part of the 2nd Division.

A 'Mobile Division' was formed out of the X Corps and was commanded by the Hanoverian, Lt General Hugh Halkett, with Captain von Sichart as chief of staff. The advance guard was made up of:

4th Infantry Brigade
 Hanoverian 3rd Light Battalion
 Brunswick 1st Battalion
 Brunswick 2nd Battalion
 Mecklenburg Jaeger section (two companies)
 Hanoverian King's Hussars (3 squadrons)
 Mecklenburg Dragoon division (2 squadrons)
 Brunswick artillery battery and pioneers

Main Body:
 1st Infantry Brigade (Hanover)
 2nd Battalion of the 4th Regiment
 1st Battalion of the 5th Regiment
 2nd Battalion of the 6th Regiment
 9 pounder Foot artillery battery

2nd Infantry Brigade
 (1st Half brigade - Mecklenburg)
 Grenadier Guard
 2nd Musketeer Battalion
 Battery of foot artillery

 (2nd Half brigade - Oldenburg)
 1st battalion of the 1st Regiment

2nd Battalion of the 1st Regiment
Battery of foot artillery

3rd Infantry Brigade (Hanover)
1st Battalion of the 2nd Regiment
2nd Battalion of the 2nd Regiment
1st Battalion of the 3rd Regiment

Reserve cavalry (Hanover)
1st Dragoons (3 squadrons)
4th Dragoons (3 squadrons)
Horse Artillery battery

Total force for the march into Holstein was 13½ battalions, 11 squadrons and 4 batteries, in all about 11,000 men.

Uniforms
Contemporary pictures or descriptions of uniforms are very rare, the following is based on best information presently available.

Hanover
Up to the accession of Queen Victoria to the throne in 1837, the Hanoverian army, though independent, had followed the English style with red coats and white lace. As the Salic law operated in Hanover which did not allow a woman to succeed, a younger son of George III, Ernest Augustus, was proclaimed king. Thus ended 123 years of personal union between England and Hanover.

In 1838 the army consisted of one Guard Regiment, one Guard Jaeger battalion, seven infantry regiments, three light battalions, three Guard cavalry regiments, one hussar regiment and four dragoon regiments. The infantry regiments were made up of two battalions each of 812 men, a cavalry regiment 418 men.

1848 was a period of change in many ways, and military dress was one part of it. At the opening of the campaign the army was still wearing the uniform adopted in 1837. Dark blue double breasted tailed coat with red collar, red round cuffs and red turnbacks. Yellow metal buttons, two rows of eight down the front and three on each cuff. Yellow lace bars were worn on each side of the collar. The shako had a bell topped felt body with leather top and peak. The shako plate was a disk embossed with a Running Horse of Hanover, surrounded by oak leaves and topped with a crown. Cords and flounders in white. The cockade was white, then yellow with a black centre. Dark grey trousers piped red, with white linen for summer wear, although some illustrations show them wearing the former light blue issue. White cross belts. The shoulder straps were white for the Guard and 1st (Life)

Regiments, red for the 2nd and 3rd Regiments, yellow for the 4th and 5th, and light blue for the 6th and 7th. The regimental number was shown on the shoulder straps. Officers wore a sash round the waist and epaulettes, straps and pads in the regimental colour with yellow metal half moons on a red pad.

The light battalions wore the same style of uniform but the basic colour was green with black facings and white metal buttons. Black cap lines, silver for officers. Cross belts black.

In campaign dress the Hanoverian army still retained the round wooden water bottle carried by all British soldiers since Napoleonic times, with the unit identified by a painted numeral on the blue body. All units wore brown cowhide packs with a steel mess tin strapped to the top. Arms were a percussion musket and bayonet with a short sword.

Artillery, again the same uniform as the infantry in blue with black facings and yellow metal buttons.

Rank badges for NCOs were similar to the Prussian service with lace round the collar and cuffs. Officers had epaulettes and a sash of silver with two yellow stripes.

The dragoons wore a similar dress to the infantry, the 1st King's Dragoons with red facings and yellow buttons and collar lace; the 2nd Leib Dragoons yellow facings and white buttons and lace; the 3rd Duke of Cambridge Dragoons, light blue facings and white buttons and lace; the 4th Crown Prince Dragoons, white facings and yellow buttons and lace. The shako was similar to the infantry. The King's Hussars wore a fur hussar cap with a red bag, blue dolman and pelisse with yellow cords, and grey overalls with red piping.

Brunswick

The Brunswick troops were famously dressed in black during the Napoleonic period, but were later reorganised and adopted the Prussian style. In 1823 the jackets were dark blue with red facings and in 1844 they were replaced by tunics in similar colours. White guard lace was worn on the collar and cuffs. The buttons were white metal. White cross belts and pack straps. Grey trousers with red piping with white linen for summer. The shako was tall, narrowing towards the top with leather square cut peak and leather bands around the base and top. The front was decorated with a 'guard star' and a light blue and yellow cockade. A black falling horse hair plume was fitted above the cockade. Brown cow skin packs with steel mess tin attached to the top. The artillery wore a similar uniform, but with yellow metal buttons and lace. They wore a black leather Bavarian style crested helmet with yellow metal fittings.

Brunswick, infantry officer

Mecklenburg, jaeger officer

Mecklenburg

In 1848 the Mecklenburg forces wore a Prussian style uniform. In 1845 the dark blue tunic with red collar and round cuffs, red piping and white shoulder straps for the Grenadier Guard, yellow for the 2nd Musketeer battalion and white metal buttons was introduced. Grey trousers piped red for winter, white for summer. White belts and straps. Black oilskin breadbag. Prussian style helmet with brass fittings, the top of the spike finished in a small ball. The jaeger had green collar, cuffs and cuff flaps all piped red and white metal buttons. They wore a black leather shako with a black falling plume and brass fittings. Straps and belts in black. Officers carried a sabre in a steel scabbard and wore a gold sash with a red and a blue stripe. The dragoons wore dark blue tunic with red collar with yellow guard lace, red round cuffs and piping. Grey riding trousers and steel spurs. Steel helmet with brass spike and fittings.

Oldenburg

In 1849 Oldenburg had four line battalions and one light. The uniform was a dark blue tunic with blue pointed cuffs piped red, red collar and red piping. Dark blue trousers piped red. Belts and straps white leather, with the pack straps attached to the belt as in Prussia. The ammunition pouch was attached to the front of the waistbelt. The leather helmet was Prussian in form with white metal fittings and chinscales. The spike was of a distinctive shape, smooth without the central disc as with Prussian and other models. The cockade under the left chinscale boss was blue with a red ring. Officers wore epaulettes and a gold sash with red and blue stripes.

In 1849 the Federal forces were reorganised for the new campaign. Some of the contingents from the X Corps Mobile division were replaced by fresh troops and many of the smaller German states provided men. Even some of the south German states, Bavaria, Baden and Wurttemberg sent a contribution to the Federal Army. The combined German Army in the duchies was commanded by the Prussian General von Prittwitz and consisted of the Schleswig-Holstein division (see that part of the chapter on the Schleswig-Holstein army for 1849) and:

1st Combined Division, Lieutenant General Prince Edward of Saxe-Altenburg (from Bavaria)

1st Brigade (Bavarian) Major General von Schmalz
    2nd Jaeger battalion
    2nd Battalion of the 4th Infantry Regiment
    1st Battalion of the 7th Infantry Regiment
    1st Battalion of the 8th Infantry Regiment
    2nd Battalion of the 13th Infantry Regiment
    5th Light Horse (six squadrons)
    Artillery section of 16 guns (6 and 12 pounders)

2nd Combined Brigade (Hessian), Major Gen von Spangenberg
2nd Battalion of the Hesse Leibgarde Regiment
2nd Battalion of the 1st Regiment
2nd Battalion of the 2nd Regiment
Hesse Rifle Battalion
Saxony-Weimar Infantry Battalion
Saxony-Altenburg Infantry Battalion
Schaumburg-Lippe Infantry Battalion (1 company)
Hesse Hussars (four squadrons)
Hesse Foot Artillery (six 6 pounder guns)
Half battery Hesse Horse Artillery (three guns)

2nd Combined Division, Major General von Wyneken (Hanover)

1st Brigade (Hanover) Major General von Ludowig
1st Battalion, Leib Regiment
1st Light Infantry Battalion
3rd Light Infantry Battalion
1st Battalion of the 3rd Regiment
1st Battalion of the 5th Regiment
Crown Prince Dragoons (4 squadrons)
Two Foot Batteries (6 pounders and 9 pounders)
One Horse Artillery Battery

2nd Brigade (Saxony) Major General von Heintze (Saxon)
2nd Infantry Regiment (3 battalions)
3rd Infantry Regiment (3 battalions)
Combined Rifle battalion
Horse Guards (4 squadrons)
12 pounder Foot Battery (8 guns)
6 pounder Foot Battery (8 guns)

3rd Division (Prussian) (see chapter on the Prussian army)

Combined Reserve Division, Lieutenant General Bauer (Hesse)

1st Combined Brigade, Duke of Nassau
Combined Nassau Infantry Regiment
(1st, 3rd and 5th Infantry Battalions)
Anhalt-Dessau Infantry Battalion
Anhalt-Bernburg-Koethen Infantry Battalion
Hesse-Homburg Infantry (one company)
Brunswick 6 pounder Artillery Battery (6 guns)

2nd Combined Brigade, Count von Rantzau (Oldenburg)
Oldenburg Infantry Regiment (1st, 2nd and 4th battalions)
Brunswick Infantry Regiment (1st and 2nd battalions)
Waldeck Infantry Battalion
Lippe-Detmold Infantry Battalion
Oldenburg 6 pounder Artillery Battery (8 guns)
Brunswick Hussars (2 squadrons)

Denmark, Infantryman, 1848. Full dress

Denmark, Jaeger, 1848-51 Field dress with peaked cap, red pack straps from old equipment

Denmark, Infantryman, 1849. Field dress, kepi and all new equipment

Denmark, Foot Guard, dress worn at the battle of Idstedt in 1850

Denmark, Artilleryman, 1849

Denmark, Dragoon 1848 field dress

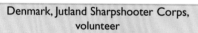
Denmark, Jutland Sharpshooter Corps,
volunteer

Schleswig-Holstein, Infantryman,
full dress

Schleswig-Holstein, Dragoon

Schleswig-Holstein, Volunteer 1848, wearing old Danish equipment.

Schleswig-Holstein, Sharpshooter of Bracklow's Volunteers

Schleswig-Holstein, Volunteer Officer, civilian dress with sash in 'German' colours

Schleswig-Holstein, German Volunteer, May 1848

Prussian, Jaeger, old equipment and carrying a hammer to ram down bullet.

Prussia, Foot Guard Grenadier Regt no. 2 'Kaiser Franz'

Prussia, Landwehrman

Federal German forces, Hanover, infantryman
1848

Federal German forces, Bavaria, infantryman
1849

Federal German forces, Nassau, artillery
officer, 1849

Federal German forces, Saxony, infantryman
1849

Federal German forces, Oldenburg, infantryman

Federal German forces, Lippe Detmold, fusilier

Scandinavia, Norway, artillery officer

Scandinavia, Sweden, infantryman

Denmark, 6th Reserve Infantry battalion

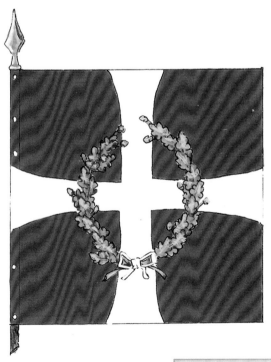

Denmark, Jutland Sharpshooters

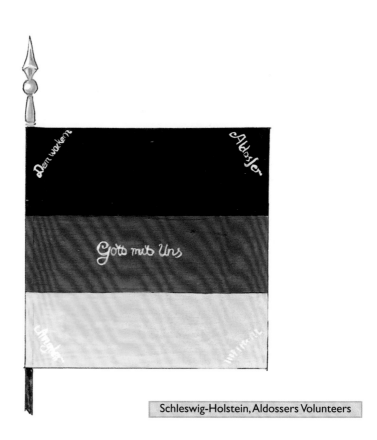

Schleswig-Holstein, Aldossers Volunteers

Schleswig-Holstein, Students company (2nd coy, 4th Freicorps)

Combined Brigade, Reserves, Duke of Saxe-Coburg-Gotha (Saxon)
  One battalion of infantry from Wurttemburg
  One battalion of infantry from Baden
  Saxony-Coburg-Gotha Infantry Battalion
  Saxony-Meiningen Infantry Battalion
  Reuss Infantry Battalion
  Hamburg Dragoons (2 squadrons)
  Nassau 6 pounder Foot Battery (6 guns)
  Hesse-Darmstadt 6 pounder Foot Battery (6 guns)

Uniforms

Bavaria

By 1848 the Bavarians had replaced the coatee with a tunic in mid blue with red shoulder straps and piping. Regiments where distinguished by coloured collar and round cuffs and the metal of the buttons. Light blue trousers also piped red. The field cap was light blue with red piping round the band and crown, it had a small black leather peak and chin strap and a small cloth badge of a crown on the front of the upper part.. The helmet was black leather with a black woollen crest and yellow metal fittings, the plate was in the shape of a sunburst with the king's monogram in the centre (M). The first two battalion in each regiment had white cross belts, the third, the scheutzen (light infantry) battalion had black, all with the cap pouch in the centre of the cross.

The jaeger battalions wore the same uniform with green collar, cuffs and shoulder straps, yellow metal buttons. Blue trousers piped green. Cross belts black.

Regiment	Collar and cuffs	Button colour
Life Regiment	Red	white
1st	Dark red	yellow
2nd	Black	yellow
3rd	Red	yellow
4th	Yellow	white
5th	Pink	white
6th	Red	white
7th	Pink	yellow
8th	Yellow	yellow
9th	Crimson	yellow
10th	Crimson	white
11th	Black	white
12th	Orange	white
13th	Dark green	white
14th	Dark green	yellow
15th	Orange	yellow

Wurttemburg,infantryman

Those regiments with black or dark green facings had them piped red.

The 5th Light Horse wore a basic infantry uniform, the helmet was strengthened by white metal bars on either side of the crown and the peak had a yellow metal edging. White plume on the right side for parade. The tunic had red collar and cuffs and yellow metal buttons. In place of shoulder straps they wore white metal shoulder scales.

The artillery wore a helmet similar to the Light Horse with a red plume for parade. The tunic and trousers were dark blue with black collar and cuffs, piped red. Yellow metal buttons. Like the Light Horse they wore shoulder scales, but in yellow metal. White cross belts.

Hesse
Hesse-Kassel took to wearing the Prussian style uniform in 1846. The tunic had a red collar and cuff flaps. The 1st Regiment had yellow shoulder straps and cuff flap piping, the 2nd white and the 3rd red, but with no cuff flap piping. The buttons were yellow metal. The Leibgarde regiment had a red collar and round cuffs, white shoulder straps, buttons and guard lace on collar and cuffs. Grey trousers piped red in winter white for summer. The helmet was black leather with yellow metal fittings and chin scales. The helmet plate for the line regiments had a Hessian crowned lion rampant clutching a sword in its right paw, the guard regiment had a silver star.
The rifle battalion (scheutzen) wore a dark green tunic with black collar and cuffs piped red. Green cuff flaps piped red. Red shoulder straps, yellow metal buttons.

The hussars were dressed in the Prussian style , the 1st Regiment in cornflower blue, the 2nd in dark blue. White lace. Grey riding trousers with red piping. They both wore a high bearskin cap with yellow metal chinscales, white cords and a red bag. On the front a Hessian oval cockade of white with a red centre.

Hanover
It is likely that the Hanoverians in 1849 wore the same uniforms as in 1848. A new style had been authorised, in the Prussian style and with the spiked helmet. It appears that only the Foot Guard and 1st Infantry regiments were issued with the new helmet, with a star burst plate for the Guard and a white metal leaping horse badge for the 1st. The artillery had a helmet topped by a ball. The plate was a leaping horse over a scroll containing the battle honours PENINSULA WATERLOO. A contemporary print shows Hanoverian troops in action at Ulderup on 6th April 1849 wearing the new tunic, but retaining the shako.

Saxony
In December 1849 the Saxon army went into the new style tunic, but for the Danish campaign it was still in the old tail coat it had worn since the early 1830's. The infantry coat was a double breasted mid green garment with

two rows of eight yellow metal buttons, light blue collar and cuffs with red piping. Green shoulder straps and turnbacks both piped red. The regimental distinctions were shown on the cuff patches, red for the Life Regiment, light blue for the 1st, white for the 2nd, green for the 3rd and black for the Garrison Division stationed in the fortress of Koenigstein. The shako was very similar to the Austrian model, narrower at the top with leather bands top and bottom, black peak and chin strap. The shako plate was a yellow metal star with a central blue plaque containing the monogram of the king in silver. Green cockade edged white. White cross belts and pack straps, with black leather percussion cap pouch on the centre of the chest.

The rifle battalions had the same uniform, only the collar and cuffs were black. The cuff patches were red for the 1st Battalion, light green for the 2nd and light blue for the 3rd. Black belts and grey trousers piped red.

Foot artillery had the same green tailed coatee with red collar and cuffs, red piping and yellow metal buttons. Buff leather belt for the short sword.

The Horse Guards wore a cornflower blue coatee and riding trousers with white collar, cuff patches and piping. Yellow metal buttons and shoulder scales. Black leather crested helmet with yellow metal fittings and black fur crest. White belts. The shabraque and blanket roll were cornflower blue with white edging.

Nassau
The yellow cross belts worn during the Napoleonic wars were still in use in 1848. The single breasted tail coats were dark green with black collars and cuffs piped orange, red turn backs, yellow metal buttons. Red shoulder rolls in full dress. Bell topped shako with a yellow metal star, red cords and flounders for parade. Dark grey trousers piped red. The artillery wore a similar uniform with a crossed canon badge on the shako, The Nassau cockade was blue with an orange edge. Officers wore yellow metal epaulettes and an orange sash. On campaign the shako was protected by an oilcloth cover. Brown cowskin pack with dark grey greatcoat rolled on top.

Anhalt
In 1846 the duchies of Anhalt adopted the Prussian style tunic in dark green with pink facings for the Dessau battalion and yellow for the Koethen battalion. The spiked helmet had a white metal plate and fittings. Grey trousers and black leather equipment.

Oldenburg
See 1848 above.

Brunswick
See 1848 above.

Baden, infantry officer

Saxony Coburg, infantryman

Waldeck
Dark green tunic with green collar, red collar patches, shoulder straps, round cuffs and piping. Yellow metal buttons. Grey trousers. The helmet was like the Prussian, but with a starburst plate in place of the eagle. Black crossbelts and pack straps.

Lippe-Detmold
Green tunics and collars with red collar patches and cuffs, yellow metal buttons. Red shoulder straps with yellow piping Black spiked helmet with rounded peak and yellow metal fittings. In the centre of the yellow metal star plate a white metal Lippe heraldic rose. This badge also appeared on the flap of the single ammunition pouch worn at the back. The Lippe cockade of red and yellow, worn under the right hand side chin scale boss, was changed to the 'German' colours of black/red/gold during the years 1848 to 1849. Black leather Prussian style straps and belts. Grey trousers with red piping.

Wurttemburg
The tunic was powder blue with red collar, shoulder straps, pointed cuffs and piping. White metal buttons. The trousers were also blue with red piping. The regimental number was shown in white on the shoulder strap. The tapering shako had a blue cloth body with a wide black leather band round the bottom and white lace around the top. On the front a red and black cockade held on with a white lace loop. On campaign it was covered in a waterproof cover with the regimental number painted in white. Crossbelts and pack straps were white.

Baden
The 1st Battalion of Infantry Regiment no. 4 was all Baden could spare to help the Schleswig-Holstein cause. The soldiers wore a large bell topped shako with a front and back peak and a large Baden griffon (a winged lion) badge on the front in yellow metal. The chin scales were also yellow. Red cockade edged yellow. Dark blue single breasted tail coat with red collar, cuffs and cuff patches. Red turnbacks. White regimental number on the shoulder straps. Dark blue trousers piped red. White cross belts supporting a short sword and cartridge pouch. On campaign the battalion wore light grey greatcoats with a small blue stand up collar and blue shoulder straps. Officers wore epaulettes without fringes and a silver sash with two red lines running through it.

Saxony-Coburg-Gotha
Dark green tunic with black collar and cuffs, piped red. Red shoulder straps. Grey trousers, white in summer. Bavarian style crested helmet with black fur crest, yellow metal fittings and a white plume. White cross belts. On campaign the battalion wore a grey greatcoat with two rows of yellow metal buttons.

Saxony-Meiningen

Dark green tunics with black collar and cuffs, red shoulder straps and cuff patches. Red piping. Yellow metal buttons. Grey trousers piped red. Black cross belts. Helmet with yellow metal fittings but a silver star plate.

Reuss

The traditional white uniform was replaced in 1845 by a black tunic with light blue collar patches, cuff patches and piping. Black trousers piped light blue in winter, white linen in summer. White cross belts. Spiked helmet with yellow metal fittings, black Austrian style kepi piped light blue for barrack dress.

Saxony-Weimar

Dark green tunic with green collar, cuffs and cuff patches, all piped in yellow. Grey trousers piped yellow in winter, white linen in summer. Double yellow lace on the collar. Yellow metal buttons. Black cross belts and pack straps. Spiked helmet with yellow metal fittings, the spike ending in a small 'turret' shape. Officers wore epaulettes and yellow sashes.

Saxony-Altenburg

In 1845 the battalion was clothed in dark blue tunics, black collars and cuffs, piped red with yellow lace loops and yellow metal buttons. Grey trousers, white cross belts. Leather spiked helmet with yellow metal star and fittings. The spike ended in a small 'turret' shape.

Schaumburg-Lippe

Dark green tunic with black collar, round cuffs and shoulder straps all piped red. Grey trousers, black cross belts. A Bavarian style helmet, black crest, brass chin scales and plate with silver coat of arms.

Hesse Homburg

Dark green tunic, carmine red piping, white buttons. Carmine red cuff patches. Prussian style spiked helmet.

Saxony Weimar, infantryman

Chapter 7
Scandinavia

Sweden and Norway had been united since the end of the Napoleonic wars under the Swedish king, but retained much of their separate government institutions including the military. There was, in effect, separate Swedish and Norwegian armies. During the August 1849 armistice a combined force was sent to the Denmark to help enforce the ceasefire. It amounted to a brigade, under the command of Major General Malmborg and was made up of:

Swedish contingent:
>One battalion of the 1st Life Grenadier Regiment
>One battalion of the Värmlog Regiment
>One battalion of the North Skanska Regiment
>Two squadrons of the Skanska Hussars
>One squadron of the Crown Prince Hussars
>One 6 pounder battery of the Wendes Artillery regiment

Norwegian contingent:
>Two companies of the Norwegian Rifle Corps
>One battalion of the Numedals Musketeers
>One section of mounted jaeger
>Half battery of the 12 pounder Sonderfield Artillery Regiment.

In all 4,500 men. This was not the total Scandinavian contribution to the war, since a number of individual Swedish volunteers joined the Danish army, many as officers and NCOs and a number were killed in action. The total number of volunteers was 243.

The Swedish army was made up of three types of units, those made up of volunteers who served for up to 14 years and formed the regular army. They numbered about 7,700 men in three regiments of infantry each of two battalions, two regiments of cavalry and three regiments of artillery, 13 Foot and four horse batteries. The second force was made up of the provincial regiments (Indelta) composed of 45 battalions of infantry and six regiments of cavalry. Lastly the Reserve, all able bodied men between the ages of 20 to 25. Apart from the regulars, the Indelta and Reserve were little better than a partly trained militia.

The Norwegians were organised differently with a regular army of 22 battalions of infantry, a regiment of artillery and a cavalry brigade, in all about 15,000 men. In support was a militia of about 9,000 men.

Uniforms

Swedish and Norwegian troops dressed in a similar fashion in dark blue single breasted tunics with coloured collar patches for Swedish regiments and red for the Norwegians

Both armies wore a leather spiked helmet, the main difference to the Prussian model being the rounded front peak. The Swedish troops had a yellow metal plate with the Swedish three crowns emblem, the Norwegian had a yellow metal heraldic lion rampant holding an axe.

The Swedish 1st Life Grenadiers had red collar patches with white guard lace, light blue shoulder straps, blue cuffs and red cuff patches. White cross belts and white trousers. The other battalions had yellow collar patches and blue cuffs and cuff patches piped yellow. Yellow metal buttons.

The Swedish hussars wore a tall shako, narrower at the top, with a leather peak at the front and at the back. Yellow cockade on the front secured by a button and a broad lace loop. Short plume consisting of a ball and tuft. Yellow over blue for the Crown Prince regiment and blue over yellow for the Skanska. Yellow cap lines and flounders. Dark blue pelisse, dolman and trousers, yellow cuffs for the Crown Prince and light blue for the Skanska. Yellow lace, cords and loops, black fur to the pelisse. Buff shoulder belt. The sabretache for both units was black decorated with the Swedish arms of three crowns, with a large crown above.

The Wendes Artillery regiment had white collar patches, otherwise uniform like the infantry apart from the helmet which had yellow metal fittings and a black woollen crest.

The Norwegian musketeers had red collar patches, white shoulder straps and yellow metal buttons. Blue cuffs piped red. Trousers dark grey piped red. White cross belts. The riflemen had dark green tunics with black collar patches, white metal buttons, green cuffs piped black.

The mounted jaeger had a shako with a crimson body black leather top and peak, cockade of white/blue/white/red secured with white lace loop. Tunic dark green with crimson collar patches and piping. Green cuffs piped crimson. White metal buttons. Trousers dark grey with crimson piping. Black belts.

The artillery had a dark blue tunic with crimson collar patches and piping, blue round cuffs piped crimson. Dark grey trousers piped crimson. Helmet like the Swedes with a yellow sunburst badge and black crest.

Chapter 8
The 1848 Campaign

At the end of March the Schleswig-Holstein army commanded in the field by Major General von Krohn, left Rendsburg and early in April were posted around the village of Bov (in Danish, known as Bau in German), to the north of Flensburg. As soon as the Schleswig-Holstein dispositions had been established the Danes planned to attack it and hopefully nip the insurrection in the bud. General Hedemann planned to hold the Schleswig-Holstein army with his main force while two flanking attacks were made against the Germans. An infantry brigade under Colonel Bülow would strike through Bov and operate against the German flank, while the cavalry brigade would swing deep to the right and then move against Flensburg itself, blocking any possible retreat.

The Battle of Bov
On the morning of 9th April, the Danish 3rd Jaegers, the 12th Line Battalion and a half battery advanced on Bov and soon captured the village. The Schleswig-Holstein troops retreated from Bov towards Niehuus and then to Harrislee. Bülow's brigade pressed on towards Flensburg where another fight took place around Neustadt. Most of the troops managed to get through Flensburg before the Danish cavalry arrived.

Other Danish units advanced against the right of the Schleswig-Holstein position around the Coppermill. This was defended by Captain Michelsen with the 2nd Schleswig-Holstein Jaegers and a company of volunteers made up of students from Kiel university. They held on despite the retreat of the rest of the Schleswig-Holstein army as General von Krohn did not send orders to withdraw. Michelsen, realising he was on his own, decided to pull back to Flensburg, but the only route was the road was next to an arm of the sea known as the Flensburg Fjord. About 500 metres from the shore stood several Danish gunboats which immediately opened fire. As they struggled to escape from the fire of the gunboats their route was blocked by a battalion from Bülow's brigade which had advanced from Harrislee. The whole of Michelsen's command were either killed or captured.

The Schleswig-Holstein army made its way back to Rendsburg in double quick time! It had suffered 30 killed and 143 wounded who were all taken prisoner, but more seriously another 780 unwounded men were captured. The Danes suffered 16 dead and 78 wounded.

It had not been an auspicious start to the war for the Schleswig-Holstein army, but had encouraged the Danes, even though they had not destroyed the insurgents. Luckily for the Schleswig-Holsteiners, when they arrived at Rendsburg they were met by a Prussian division of 12,000 men and a Federal

German division of 10,000 drawn from Hanover, Mecklenburg and Brunswick. Behind this screen the Schleswig-Holstein army was reorganised and recruited up to 9,000 men.

The Battle of Schleswig, 23rd April

The newly arrived Prussians and federal Germans under the Prussian general Wrangel, determined to make their presence felt and advanced in two columns towards the city of Schleswig. However the Prussian commander did not wait for all his troops to arrive but advanced with about 20,000 men. Just to the south of Schleswig it met the Danish army about 12,000 strong. One of the Prussian columns became engaged with the Danes while to other was executing a flank march. The Danes thus had an advantage of numbers in that part of the field and fell back slowly against Prussian pressure until they deemed it the right moment for a counter-attack as the Prussians were becoming dispersed. An unfortunate series of incidents, confusion 'the fog of war' now intervened and the moment passed. The Danes withdrew as night fell, but felt that they had given a good account of themselves.

Battle of Oversee, 24th April

The day after the fighting at Schleswig the Danish command decided to gave their men twenty four hours rest. At the same time Wrangel ordered up the federal troops to pursue the retreating Danes. At Oversee the Danish outposts were surprised and overwhelmed and panic set in, order was only restored with difficulty.

Duppel, 28th May

The following month the Danes took the offensive against the Federal German troops around Duppel with the intention of driving them away from their positions overlooking the Als Sound and the Danish bridgehead on the mainland at Sundeved. Fourteen thousand soldiers crossed the Sound against the 7,000 men commanded by the Hanoverian general, Halkett. By evening the Danes had achieved their objectives.

Wrangel determined to regain lost ground and launched a counter-attack on 5th June with the Federal troops supported by two Prussian brigades together with the Schleswig-Holstein army. The Danes fought back, the Guards supported by a chasseur battalion and two line battalions, forcing the Prussians to retreat.

The pressure by foreign governments, mainly Russia and Great Britain, brought about a ceasefire on 26th August which lasted for seven months during which time an agreement could hopefully be reached.

Chapter 9
The 1849 Campaign

Divisions within the Danish government ensured that the peace talks came to nothing. In March 1849 they brought the cease fire to an end and on the 3rd April the war resumed. Both sides had used the time to build up their forces, the Danish army numbered 41,000 men and the Schleswig-Holstein army commanded by the Prussian Edward von Bonin, 14,000 with a further 5,000 in reserve. The Federal army, made up of contingents from 23 states, totalled 46,700 men under General von Prittwitz.

The Danes took the initiative and planned an invasion of Schleswig in two columns, one from Jutland and the other from the island of Alsen, uniting just to north of Flensburg, where the Schleswig-Holstein army was stationed. The object was to destroy the Schleswig-Holsteiners before the Federal army, based in the duchy Holstein, could come to its rescue. Disagreements between the Danish minister of war and the High Command led to changes in the plan, the minister advocating a sea born assault on the town of Schleswig. This was later reduced to a naval demonstration against the defences at Eckernforde.

The land forces marched into the duchy of Schleswig and in a series of successful skirmishes arrived in the Flensburg. However, the Danish navy in its attempt to silence the shore batteries in Eckernforde, by a number of errors ended up losing the battleship *Christian VIII* which blew up after being set on fire with red hot shot and the frigate *Gefion* which surrendered after being reduced almost to a hulk.

As a consequence, Hansen, the Danish Minister of War ordered the army to retreat to its original positions and replaced the army commander and chief of staff with his own nominees. The Schleswig-Holstein army, led by Bonin, gleefully followed the Danes, and although ordered not to crossed into Jutland and captured Kolding. Although the Danes counterattacked and took back the town, they had to give it up after being pressed by superior numbers.

This success put pressure on the Federal army to invade Jutland and in May the German forces advanced into the peninsula, some of the Danes retiring to the island of Als, a large number into the fortress of Fredericia an the remainder to positions further north. The Schleswig-Holstein army undertook to lay siege to Fredericia. On 6th July the Danish garrison, reinforced to 19,000 men (they could move their troops by sea without interference), made a sortie and in a series of bloody fights forced the Schleswig-Holsteiners away from the fortress. They also captured their siege supplies and over 30 guns.

During the fighting Danish diplomats had been in negotiation with the Prussian government to bring about another ceasefire which could be used as the basis of an agreement to end the war. The ceasefire was signed on 10th July. The talks lasted for a year, with the Prussians, the Federal German parliament and the Danes all demanding special conditions for peace, with the Schleswig-Holsteiners not agreeing with any of them. Prussia finally accepted a peace treaty , but one which did not address any of the problems that gave rise to the war in the first place.

Danish infantry in action 1848.

Chapter 10
The 1850 Campaign

After being deserted by their Prussian allies the Schleswig-Holsteiners did not give up hope, but determined to continue the fight on their own. Political considerations demanded that they take the initiative and on 14th July the whole army, amounting to 30,000 men now commanded by a former general in the Prussian service Willisen, marched into the Duchy of Schleswig. On the 16th the Danish army, now augmented to 37,000 men cautiously entered Schleswig from the north. By the 25th the two armies came into contact around the town of Idstedt.

The ground was very broken with lakes, streams and marshes making co-operation between different units extremely difficult. The result was a bitter fight between individual brigades and divisions with neither side being able to bring decisive numbers into action against opposing formations. Again, lack of communications hindered action which could have brought about victory. A flanking march by a Danish brigade was ordered back just as it was about to take the Schleswig-Holsteiners in the rear because of a difficult situation on the other wing of the army which had resolved itself several hours before.

Danish post in winter

Danish stretcher bearers.

The Schleswig-Holsteiners took the opportunity to withdraw. It had been a bloody fight with heavy casualties on both sides. The army of the duchies retreated into Holstein, slowly followed by the Danes who reoccupied their old positions on the Dannewerk*. Again political pressure by the Schleswig-Holstein government forced the army onto the offensive and on 12th September they attacked part of the Danish position at Missunde. The Danish brigade defending the place being well supplied with artillery, repulsed the attack.

Willisen tried again on 29th September against the town of Friedrichstadt. He bombarded the town for several days before making a night assault. Fighting, much of it at close quarters, continue into the following morning, before he reluctantly called off the attack.

Intense political pressure was applied to the Schleswig-Holstein government to come to terms, but as that meant capitulation to the Danes they determined to fight on. Willisen was replaced by General von der Horst who on 31st December again unsuccessfully attacked the Missunde position.

With both Austria and Prussia demanding an end to the war the Schleswig-Holstein government accepted that they could not continue and in January 1851 brought back the army into Holstein and began to disband it.

*This was an early medieval earthwork built by the Danes to keep the Germans out of the Jutland peninsula. It began just south of the town of Schleswig on the Baltic coast and stretched across to the North Sea.

Chapter 11
Postscript

The Danish troops marched into the duchies and the Schleswig-Holsteiners were forced to dismantle their government, army and navy. The Treaty of London, signed on 8 May 1852 by Great Britain, Russia, Austria, France, Prussia and Sweden, guaranteed the Danish monarch in his possessions, and the rights of the German Confederation over Holstein. The duke of Augustenburg was compensated with a cash settlement. The Estates of the two duchies remained in being, controlled by the Danes, but by repressive measures and harsh treatment they failed to win over the defeated parties. The stage was set for further trouble which Prince Otto von Bismarck made full use of in 1864.

Living off the land.

Chapter 12
The Navies

The Danes great strength lay in their navy. At no time during the war did they loose command of the sea. They could move troops by water at will and maintained a blockade of the German coast seriously damaging local and international trade. In 1848 the Danish sailing navy had on commission four battle ships of 84 guns each, the Skjold, the Frederick the Sixth the Christian the Seventh and the Valdemar, and an older vessel the Danmark which carried 66 guns. Eight frigates carrying from 40 to 60 guns, supplemented by four corvettes of 20 to 28 guns, four smaller brigs of a dozen or so guns and half a dozen schooners and cutters. During the 1840's work began on a steam navy and in 1848 four ships of various sizes and armaments joined the fleet, the largest, the Hekla, was powered by a 200 horse power engine carrying two 60 pounders and four 24 pounders, the smallest, the Aegir had an 80 horse power engine and carried two 18 pounders. To support the army there were a number of oar powered gunboats that could work their way close inshore and give covering fire from their single forward pointing gun, they also carried a smaller gun in the stern. The Danes had developed and used these small inshore craft since the Napoleonic wars and they proved eminently suited to providing close support to troops operating near to the shore.

The Schleswig-Holsteiners had no naval force to counter the Danes, but immediately set about forming their own marine service. They first commandeered four ships in Schleswig-Holstein harbours, three paddle steamers and a schooner and armed them with whatever they could find, the largest with an 84 pounder gun supplemented with a 60 pounder and two 30 pounders, the smallest craft with a single 18 pounder and two 12 pounder short carronades. Secondly the government ordered a number of gunboats from local shipyards. The first boat was given the name Von der Tann in honour of the Bavarian Frei Korps commander. It was driven by a 36 horsepower engine linked to a propeller in the stern, the first ship of the type to be built in Germany. It was armed with two 60 pounder guns and four 4 pounder swivel guns and the whole weighing 120 tons.

A further 11 sailing gunboats joined the establishment during 1848 and 1849, armed with two 60 pounders. A few other odd vessels joined the fleet as and when they could be obtained, but none odder than the Firediver or Iron Sealion a submarine invented and built by an ex-NCO of the Bavarian army, Wilhelm Bauer. This had a crew of three men, two to drive the hand crank connected to the propeller and one to steer it towards its target so that it could fix an explosive device and then back off to safety.

This was the theory at any rate, in practice there were still some technical

Danish sailor on shore duty.

difficulties to overcome, but the mere threat that the vessel posed was enough to keep the Danish fleet away from Kiel harbour! On its second voyage in February 1851 Bauer took it down too deeply and it eventually hit the sea floor at 60 feet and stayed there. Only by letting in more water to equalise the pressure could Bauer and the crew open the scuttles and swim to the surface. The boat itself remained in the mud until 1887 when it was raised and taken to the Naval School at Kiel, ending up in the Berlin Naval Museum. Bauer went on to design bigger and better submarines and even built one for the Russian government during the Crimean war. This, named the Sea Devil proved to be quite successful and with its crew of 12 men made over 130 trial runs. Unfortunately the 134th run ended like the Firediver's second and it got stuck in the mud. Bauer escaped again and continued to develop other projects but ultimately failed through lack of backers.

To complicate matters, the Federal German parliament in Frankfort was persuaded that they also needed a navy. As its first admiral it chose Karl Brommy. He had started life as Bromme, went to sea at eighteen and served on a number of US vessels; as a result he altered the spelling of his name to match its English pronunciation. In 1820 during a voyage to South America he became caught up in the revolts against Spain. He signed up as a midshipman in the Chilean navy and came to the attention of its commander, Lord Cochrane. He was soon given a ship of his own, an 18 gun brigantine. When Cochrane left Chile to go to Brazil in 1822, Brommy followed him. Later he moved with his mentor to Greece and participated in the Battle of Navarino. After returning to Germany he became bored with the life of a landlubber and when the opportunity arose he accompanied Prince Otto of Bavaria who was selected to be the first king of an independent Greece. Brommy was rewarded with a senior rank in the new Greek navy. Back in Germany in 1848 Brommy campaigned to have a German navy and in March 1849 he was made commander in chief of the North Sea Flotilla.

He immediately set about organising a fleet to command! He ended up with nine steam powered ships, two sailing vessels and 27 small gunboats. He established his headquarters at the Oldenburg town of Brake, on the river Weser, between Bremen and the North Sea. His flagship was the Barbarossa, a paddle steam frigate, Glasgow built and mounting nine 68 pounder guns. On the 4th June 1849 the only action of the war involving the navy of the Federal German government (as opposed to the Schleswig-Holstein navy) took place when Brommy tried to engage the Danish sailing frigate, the Valkyrien and the steamer Gejser who were on blockade duty and came within canon shot of British territorial waters around Helgoland (Britain at the time having sovereignty over the island) so the action had to be broken off.

The Barbarossa together with two converted paddle steamers from the North Sea trade, the Lubeck, carrying one 84 pounder, one 32 pounder and four 18 pounder carronades and the smaller Hamburg with a similar armament engaged the Danish ships but with only a few casualties on each side no one could claim a victory, although the Danish blockade was maintained without interruption.

The Frankfort parliament had by an oversight forgotten to inform the largest maritime nation, Great Britain, that their ships sailed under the 'black, red, gold' war flag so were in danger of being treated as pirates. This more or less put an end to the activities of the new born German navy. In 1852 the navy was disbanded and the fleet sold off by auction.

Uniforms

Uniforms for the world's navies was in its infancy in 1848, but most of the world copied the largest and most powerful navy, that of Great Britain. Officers of Danish, Schleswig-Holstein or German navies would be difficult to distinguish, all wore dark blue, or black frock coats with various amounts of gold lace according to rank. White shirts and black ties were also common. Headwear was a blue peaked cap. For sailors the same remarks apply, blue short jackets, white trousers and straw hats were universal. The sailors of the Schleswig-Holstein navy wore a round field cap, similar to the army, in dark blue with a band round the lower part showing the ship's name, ie KANONENBOOT No.1.

Danish Battleship Christian VIII and frigate Gefion

Bibliography:

There is very little published in English on the 'Three Year's War' and it is generally mentioned only as an afterthought when referring to the European revolutions of 1848. This is hardly surprising when you consider what else was happening at the same time. There seems to be renewed interest in Germany and a new book on the Schleswig-Holstein army has recently been published.

Some of the sources used in this booklet are:

- *Chakoten*, the journal of the Danish wargaming and military history society.
- Holst, Frits og Larsen, Axel, *Felttogene I Vore Første Frihedsaar*, Kjøbenhavn, 1888
- Knötel, Richard and Knötel, Herbert and Sieg, Herbert, *Uniforms of the World*, (translation of *Handbuch der Uniformenkunde*, Hamburg 1937) London, 1980
- Nielsen, Johs., *The Schleswig-Holstein Revolt 1848-1850*, Copenhagen 1993
- Schlürmann, Jan, *Die Schleswig-Holsteinische Armee 1848-1851*, Tönning 2004
- Stoltz, Gerd, *Der Kampf um Friedrichstadt im Jahre 1850*, Husum, 2000
- Stoltz, Gerd, *Die Schleswig-Holsteinische Armee von 1848/51*, Eckernförde, 1978
- Stoltz, Gerd, *Die schleswig-holsteinische Erhebung*, Husum, 1996
- Stoltz, Gerd, *Die Schleswig-Holsteinische Marine 1848-1852*, Heide,1987
- Walbom-Pramvig, Børge, *Uniformer, Faner og Våben*, 1988

www.milhist.dk Danish military history website

Information on the volunteer units and uniforms of both Danish and Schleswig-Holstein armies from unpublished sources via Stuart Penhall.

Notes on the Federal German navy from Raun Kristensen via Rob Morgan.